ACID ATTACK

MALEDICTION IN INDIA

PUSHPITA TRIPATHI

Made with ♥ on the Notion Press Platform
www.notionpress.com

This book is dedicated to my beloved parents..,

Shri Pradeep Kumar Tripathi
&
Mrs. Archana Tripathi

Contents

Contents

Preface

Acid attacks are one of the most heinous forms of violence that exist in our world today. These attacks involve the deliberate use of corrosive substances to disfigure, maim, and often blind victims, leaving them with lifelong physical, emotional, and psychological scars. Acid attacks are a global problem, and the majority of victims are women and girls. This violence is an expression of patriarchy and misogyny, and it is fueled by the objectification of women, toxic masculinity, and the glorification of violence in our society.

As a society, we must recognize the gravity of this issue and take concrete steps towards preventing such attacks and providing support and justice to the survivors. This book aims to shed light on the various facets of acid attacks, including the causes, consequences, and the legal and social frameworks surrounding these incidents.

The first section of the book provides an overview of the phenomenon of acid attacks, including the history of these attacks, their prevalence around the world, and the reasons why they are used as a form of violence. It explores the various types of acid used in these attacks, their accessibility, and the devastating physical and emotional impact they have on victims.

The second section of the book is dedicated to the stories of survivors. Their experiences provide insight into the emotional and psychological trauma of surviving such violence, and the hurdles they face in accessing medical, legal, and social services. Their stories are powerful reminders of the human cost of acid attacks, and they highlight the urgent need for better support systems for survivors.

This book delves into the root causes of acid attacks, including gender-based violence, patriarchy, and the prevalence of harmful cultural practices. It explores the ways in which gender inequality and discrimination perpetuate the use of acid attacks as a form of violence, and it argues for a comprehensive approach that addresses the systemic causes of this phenomenon.

The book explores the legal and policy frameworks that are in place to address acid attacks, including the legal systems of India. It also explores the role of civil society organizations in supporting survivors and advocating for change, and the importance of education and awareness-raising campaigns in preventing acid attacks.

It is my hope that this book will serve as a call to action for individuals, communities, and policymakers to address this issue with urgency and empathy. We must work together to create a world where no one has to live in fear of being targeted in such a brutal and senseless attack. We must also work to change the cultural and societal norms that enable such violence to exist. We hope that this book will contribute to this important work, and we dedicate it to the survivors of acid attacks and all those working to prevent and respond to this violence.

Author...,

Acknowledgements

Dear **Readers,**

As I present to you my book, "**Acid Attack : Malediction in India**". I would like to take a moment to express my deepest gratitude to those who have supported me throughout this journey.

First and foremost, I would like to thank the survivors of acid attacks your courage and resilience have inspired me to shed light on this heinous crime and work towards a safer and more just society. I would also like to thank the activists, organizations, and lawyers who tirelessly fight for the rights of acid attack survivors. Your dedication and passion have motivated me to delve deeper into the issue and strive for change.

My sincere thanks go to my family and friends, who have always been my pillars of strength and support. Your encouragement and belief in me have been invaluable.

Last but not least, I would like to express my gratitude to my publisher, who believed in my work and helped bring it to fruition.

To all those who have contributed in some way to the making of this book, I offer my heartfelt appreciation.

Sincerely,

Pushpita Tripathi

1

Introduction

Acid attacks are one of the most heinous forms of violence against women in India. The use of acid as a weapon to disfigure, maim or kill a person is a terrifying reality for many women in the country. The number of reported cases of acid attacks in India has increased dramatically over the past decade, and it is estimated that at least one woman is attacked with acid every day in India. The reasons behind the increase in acid attacks are complex and multifaceted, including issues of gender inequality, lack of legal and social protections, and a culture of impunity that allows perpetrators to go unpunished.

The impact of acid attacks on the victims is devastating. Women who survive acid attacks are left with lifelong physical and psychological scars. They often lose their sight, hearing, and ability to speak or eat. They suffer from chronic pain, infections, and disfigurement, and are often ostracized by their communities. Many are unable to work, get married, or have children, and are forced to live in poverty.

Despite the severity of acid attacks, the legal response in India has been inadequate. Acid attacks were not recognized as a separate offence under the Indian Penal Code until 2013, and even now, the punishment for perpetrators is relatively lenient. The lack of a comprehensive legal framework to deal with acid attacks has left victims and their families without recourse and has allowed perpetrators to act with impunity.

Moreover, the social stigma attached to acid attack survivors is also a significant issue in India. The victims are often blamed for the attacks, and their families are ostracized by society. Even after recovery, they face discrimination in education, employment, and marriage. As a result, many survivors feel ashamed and isolated, leading to psychological trauma.

To address the issue, a multi-pronged approach is necessary. The government needs to strengthen the legal framework for acid attacks and ensure swift and severe punishment for perpetrators. It is also essential to provide adequate medical and psychological support to survivors. Society also needs to be educated about the issue, and steps must be taken to address the root causes of gender inequality and violence against women.

Acid attacks are a severe form of violence against women in India, and it is imperative to address this issue with urgency. The government, civil society, and the public at large must work together to provide a safe and just society for all women. Only by raising awareness and changing attitudes towards women can we hope to eliminate this form of violence from our society.

- **Meaning of Acid & Attack by Acid: -**

Acid is a chemical substance that has a pH value of less than 7. It is a highly corrosive and reactive substance that can cause severe damage to living tissues. There are several types of acids, including hydrochloric acid, sulfuric acid, and nitric acid. Acids can be found in a wide range of products and substances, including batteries, cleaning agents, and laboratory chemicals.

An acid attack is a form of violent assault in which an individual is deliberately targeted with acid. The attacker throws acid on the victim's face and body, causing severe burns and disfigurement. Acid attacks can cause permanent scarring, blindness, and even death. The use of acid as a weapon is a particularly heinous form of violence, as the physical and psychological damage inflicted on the victim is often permanent.

The reasons for acid attacks can vary, but they are often linked to issues of gender-based violence. In many cases, acid attacks are carried out against women who have rejected a man's advances, or who have defied cultural norms or family expectations. Acid attacks can also be used as a tool of revenge, intimidation, or coercion.

The impact of an acid attack on the victim is devastating. Survivors of acid attacks often suffer from physical and psychological trauma that can last a lifetime. The injuries caused by an acid attack can be life-changing, and can result in the loss of eyesight, hearing, or the ability to speak. The victim may suffer from chronic pain, infection, and disfigurement, and may be unable to work, get married, or have children. In addition to physical injuries, acid attack survivors also face social stigma and discrimination, which can compound their trauma.

The legal and social response to acid attacks has been inadequate in many countries, including India. Acid attacks were not recognized as a separate offence under the Indian Penal Code until 2013, and even now, the punishment for perpetrators is relatively lenient. The lack of a comprehensive legal framework to deal with acid attacks has left victims and their families without recourse, and has allowed perpetrators to act with impunity.

To address the issue of acid attacks, it is necessary to strengthen the legal framework for acid attacks and ensure swift and severe punishment for perpetrators. In addition, it is essential to provide adequate medical and psychological support to survivors. The society also needs to be educated about the issue, and steps must be taken to address the root causes of gender inequality and violence against women.

- **Who are accused & Victim** :

The accused in acid attack cases are often men who are known to the victim. The attacks are usually carried out as a form of retaliation, revenge, or as punishment for the victim rejecting the perpetrator's advances or defying their expectations. The attackers are often driven by a desire to cause lasting physical and psychological harm to their victims, and the use of acid as a weapon is seen as an effective means of achieving this goal.

Victims of acid attacks are primarily women, although men can also be victims. Women are often targeted because they are seen as more vulnerable and easy to control. They may be targeted for a variety of reasons, including refusing marriage proposals, ending a relationship, or resisting sexual advances. In some cases, acid attacks are carried out as part of a larger campaign of violence, including domestic abuse or harassment.

The impact of an acid attack on the victim is devastating. Survivors of acid attacks often suffer from physical and psychological trauma that can last a lifetime. The injuries caused by an acid attack can be life-changing and can result in the loss of eyesight, hearing, or the ability to speak. The victim may suffer from chronic pain, infection, and disfigurement, and may be unable to work, get married, or have children. In addition to physical injuries, acid attack survivors also face social stigma and discrimination, which can compound their trauma.

It is important to note that not all acid attacks are the result of personal vendettas. In some cases, acid attacks may be carried out as part of organized crime, such as extortion or intimidation. Victims of such attacks may be targeted randomly or for their perceived wealth or status. In such cases, the accused may be part of a criminal organization or gang.

Regardless of the reasons for an acid attack, the impact on the victim is severe and long-lasting. It is imperative to address the root causes of this violence and ensure that perpetrators are held accountable for their actions. Survivors of acid attacks need to be provided with adequate medical and psychological support, as well as legal protection to seek justice and rebuild their lives.

- **Women are an important part of our society but still, the strongest gender is male (that we called a male Dominating Society).**

Women are indeed an important part of our society, and their contributions are vital for the progress and development of any nation. However, despite the significant strides made in recent years toward gender equality, women continue to face various forms of discrimination and inequality. One of the most prevalent forms of discrimination is the male dominating society, where men hold the majority of the power and resources.

A male dominating society refers to a social structure where men hold a disproportionate share of power, privilege, and influence, both in the public and private spheres. This dominance manifests itself in various ways, such as in political representation, educational and economic opportunities, and cultural norms and practices. In many societies, men have traditionally held the highest positions of power, and women's roles have been relegated to subordinate and supportive roles.

The male dominating society has been perpetuated by deep-rooted patriarchal beliefs and cultural norms that assign men a higher status and authority than women. This has led to the systematic marginalization of women and the exclusion of their voices and perspectives from decision-making processes. The unequal distribution of power and resources has resulted in various forms of gender-based violence, including sexual harassment, domestic abuse, and honor killings.

The male dominating society has a detrimental effect on women's physical, mental, and emotional well-being. It also limits women's potential and opportunities to reach their full potential. Therefore, it is essential to challenge and transform the social norms and beliefs that perpetuate this dominance. This requires collective efforts from all members of society, including men and women, to promote gender equality and empower women to take their rightful place in society.

Therefore while men and women both have important roles to play in society, the male dominating society has perpetuated the marginalization and discrimination of women. We must strive to create a more equal and just society where everyone, regardless of gender, has an equal opportunity to succeed and reach their full potential.

- **Gender based violence :**

Gender-based violence is a form of violence that is directed towards an individual or group based on their gender identity. It includes physical, sexual, and psychological abuse, as well as economic and social discrimination. This type of violence disproportionately affects women and girls, although men and boys can also be victims.

Gender-based violence can occur in various settings, including the home, workplace, schools, and public spaces. It is perpetuated by deeply ingrained social norms and beliefs that assign different roles and expectations to men and women. Such norms often perpetuate the idea that men are superior and have the right to control and dominate women.

The impact of gender-based violence on individuals and communities is devastating. It can lead to physical injuries, mental health issues, and in extreme cases, death. Victims of gender-based violence may suffer from trauma, low self-esteem, and isolation, which can have long-term effects on their well-being and ability to participate in society.

Efforts to address gender-based violence require comprehensive measures that include prevention, protection, and access to justice for survivors. Prevention measures involve changing social norms, educating individuals and communities on the harmful effects of gender-based violence, and promoting gender equality. Protection measures include providing safe spaces and services for victims, such as shelters, hotlines, and legal aid. Access to justice measures involve holding perpetrators accountable for their actions, including legal sanctions and rehabilitation programs.

Gender-based violence is a serious violation of human rights that has a devastating impact on individuals, families, and communities. It is essential to promote gender equality and change social norms that perpetuate violence against women and girls. Comprehensive measures that address prevention, protection, and access to justice are necessary to end gender-based violence and ensure a safe and just society for all.

2

Laws Related to Acid Attacks

In India, acid attacks are considered a heinous crime, and various laws and regulations have been enacted to prevent and punish such offenses.

The following are the main laws related to acid attacks in India:

- **Indian Penal Code (IPC):** Acid attacks are considered a serious offense in India, and the Indian Penal Code (IPC) has provisions that deal specifically with acid attacks. Section 326A of the IPC defines an acid attack as the act of causing permanent or partial damage or deformity to a person's body using any corrosive substance.

According to section 326A, anyone who commits an acid attack shall be punished with imprisonment for a term ranging from ten years to life imprisonment and a fine. Additionally, section 326B deals with attempted acid attacks, and offenders may be imprisoned for up to seven years and fined.

The IPC also has provisions for other related offenses, such as criminal intimidation, causing hurt, and grievous hurt. The punishment for these offenses depends on the severity of the injury caused.

In addition to the IPC, the Criminal Law Amendment Act 2013 provides stricter punishment for acid attacks, including life imprisonment and a fine. It also mandates that hospitals provide free medical treatment to acid attack survivors.

Overall, the Indian Penal Code and other related laws provide a legal framework for the prevention and punishment of acid attacks in India. However, the proper implementation and enforcement of these laws are crucial to ensure that acid attack survivors receive the protection and support they need.

- **Criminal Law Amendment Act 2013:**

The Criminal Law Amendment Act 2013 is a law that provides stricter punishment for various crimes against women, including acid attacks. The act amended the Indian Penal Code (IPC), the Indian Evidence Act, and the Code of Criminal Procedure.

The amendment to the IPC introduced Section 326A, which deals with acid attacks. The section states that anyone who causes permanent or partial damage or deformity to a person's body using any corrosive substance, including acid, shall be punished with imprisonment for a term ranging from ten years to life imprisonment and a fine. In cases where the attack leads to the death of the victim, the offender may be given the death penalty or life imprisonment.

The amendment also mandates that hospitals provide free medical treatment to acid attack survivors. The victims are entitled to receive treatment, including plastic surgery and post-operative care, as long as they require it.

Furthermore, the law made amendments to the Indian Evidence Act, allowing statements made by the victim of a sexual assault or acid attack to be admissible in court as evidence, even if the victim dies or is unable to appear in court.

Overall, the Criminal Law Amendment Act 2013 provides stricter punishment for acid attacks and other crimes against women. It also mandates that hospitals provide free medical treatment to survivors of acid attacks, which is a significant step towards ensuring the well-being of victims.

- **The Acid Attacks and Victims Protection Bill 2017:**

The Acid Attacks and Victims Protection Bill 2017 is a proposed law aimed at providing comprehensive support and protection to acid attack survivors in India. The bill was introduced in the Rajya Sabha, the upper house of the Indian Parliament, in April 2017.

The main objectives of the bill are to prevent acid attacks, provide support and rehabilitation to victims, and ensure that offenders are brought to justice. The bill includes provisions for medical treatment, compensation, rehabilitation, and legal aid to acid attack survivors.

The bill mandates the creation of a fund for acid attack survivors, which will be used to provide financial assistance for their treatment and rehabilitation. The bill also proposes the creation of a Central Bureau of Investigation (CBI) cell to investigate acid attack cases and ensure speedy trials.

Furthermore, the bill aims to regulate the sale of acid, which is a common weapon used in acid attacks. It proposes that acid can only be sold to people who have a valid license and that the sellers maintain a record of the sale of acid. Additionally, the bill provides for stringent punishment for offenders and introduces the death penalty for cases where the victim dies due to an acid attack.

Overall, the Acid Attacks and Victims Protection Bill 2017 is a significant step towards providing comprehensive support and protection to acid attack survivors in India. The bill aims to prevent such attacks, provide support to the victims, and ensure that the offenders are brought to justice.

- **The Supreme Court guidelines:**

Acid attacks are a horrific form of violence against women that has been increasingly prevalent in India. In an effort to address this issue, the Supreme Court of India issued guidelines in July 2013 to regulate the sale of acid and provide better support and rehabilitation to the victims.

The guidelines are comprehensive and aim to address various aspects of acid attacks. One of the most critical provisions of the guidelines is the regulation of the sale of acid. The guidelines prohibit the sale of acid to minors and require sellers to maintain records of the sale, including the details of the buyer. This is an essential step in ensuring that the acid does not end up in the wrong hands and is used for the intended purposes only.

The guidelines also mandate compensation to the victims of acid attacks. This compensation includes medical treatment, rehabilitation, and monetary compensation. The amount of compensation varies depending on the severity of the attack and the losses suffered by the victim. This is an essential step in supporting the victims and helping them get back on their feet.

Another important provision of the guidelines is the recommendation for the establishment of fast-track courts to ensure speedy trials in acid attack cases. These courts are expected to complete the trials within three months of the case being registered. This is crucial in ensuring that justice is served and the offenders are punished.

Rehabilitation is another critical aspect of the guidelines. The guidelines recommend that the state governments provide free medical treatment to the victims of acid attacks, including plastic surgery and post-operative care. Additionally, the victims are recommended to be provided with vocational training and employment opportunities to help them lead a normal life.

Supreme Court guidelines are a significant step in addressing the issue of acid attacks in India. The guidelines provide a comprehensive framework for regulating the sale of acid, supporting the victims, and ensuring that the offenders are brought to justice. However, the implementation of the guidelines is essential for their success, and it requires the cooperation of the government, civil society, and the public at large. By working together, we can eliminate this form of violence from our society and provide a safe and just society for all women.

These laws and guidelines are intended to provide a legal framework for the prevention and punishment of acid attacks in India. However, the effectiveness of these laws depends on their proper implementation and enforcement. It is important to create awareness among the public and law enforcement agencies to ensure that acid attack survivors receive the protection and support they deserve.

- **Acid Attacks & Prevention Acts , 2008**

The Acid Attacks and Prevention Act, 2008 was introduced in India to address the rising number of acid attacks on women. The act aims to regulate the sale of acid and provide relief and rehabilitation to victims.

The act is a comprehensive legal framework that covers all aspects of acid attacks. It includes the definition of an acid attack and the punishment for offenders. The act provides for imprisonment of a term not less than 10 years and may extend to life imprisonment in case of serious injury. The fine can be up to INR 10 lakh, and the punishment for throwing acid could lead to imprisonment of up to seven years.

The act also provides for a mechanism to regulate the sale of acid, which is often used as a weapon in these attacks. It is mandatory to maintain records of the sale of acid, including the details of the buyer. The act also requires acid to be sold only to individuals who have a valid identity card and specifies the quantity of acid that can be sold to a single person. It prohibits the sale of acid to minors.

The act also mandates compensation to victims of acid attacks. The state government is responsible for the rehabilitation and compensation of victims. The amount of compensation varies based on the extent of the injury, and it includes medical treatment, rehabilitation, and monetary compensation. The act also provides for the setting up of a rehabilitation fund to help the victims recover and lead a normal life.

Section 3 of the Acid Attacks and Prevention Act, 2008 defines the offence of acid attack and prescribes strict punishment for the offenders. The provision aims to deter individuals from committing such heinous crimes and provide justice to the victims of acid attacks.

Overall, the Acid Attacks and Prevention Act, 2008 is an important step towards addressing the issue of acid attacks in India. The act provides a comprehensive framework to regulate the sale of acid, punish the offenders, and provide relief and rehabilitation to the victims. However, the implementation of the act is critical for its success, and it requires the cooperation of the government, civil society, and the public at large. By working together, we can eliminate this form of violence from our society and provide a safe and just society for all women.

- **Definition of acid attacks given by the National Commission of India, July 2009:**

The National Commission for Women (NCW) in India issued a definition of acid attacks in July 2009. According to this definition, acid attacks are a form of violence, where acid is thrown or poured on a person with the intention of causing harm or disfiguration. The acid is usually thrown on the face or the body of the victim, causing severe burns, injuries, and permanent disfigurement.

The definition further states that acid attacks are a gendered crime, and women are disproportionately affected by it. Acid attacks are used as a means of controlling and subjugating women, often in cases where the women have rejected the advances of men or have stood up against societal norms and patriarchal structures.

The definition also recognizes that acid attacks cause not only physical harm but also psychological and emotional trauma to the victim. The stigma and discrimination faced by acid attack survivors in society further exacerbate the impact of the crime.

The National Commission of India's definition of acid attacks highlights the severity of this heinous crime and its gendered nature.

- **Permanent disfigurement of head & face:**

Permanent disfigurement of the head and face is a devastating consequence of acid attacks. The corrosive nature of the acid causes severe burns, often resulting in permanent scarring and disfigurement. The victim's face is the most commonly targeted area in acid attacks, as it is the most visible and often the most valued feature in one's appearance.

The physical consequences of such disfigurement are accompanied by severe emotional and psychological trauma. Acid attack survivors often face social stigmatization, discrimination, and ostracism due to their disfigurement, leading to isolation, depression, and anxiety. The emotional and psychological impact of the attack can be long-lasting and can prevent survivors from leading normal lives and pursuing their dreams.

The severity of the disfigurement and the associated emotional trauma often require long-term medical treatment, including reconstructive surgeries, skin grafting, and psychological counseling. However, such treatments can be expensive, and many survivors cannot afford them. The disfigurement can also impact their employment opportunities and further exacerbate their financial difficulties.

- **Loss of eyesight:** Loss of eyesight is a severe consequence of acid attacks, and it is one of the most devastating outcomes for the victim. The corrosive nature of the acid can cause severe burns, often resulting in blindness or partial vision loss. The acid can burn through the cornea, resulting in corneal damage, and it can cause long-term damage to the retina and optic nerve.

The loss of eyesight has a profound impact on the victim's quality of life, and it can result in severe physical, emotional, and psychological trauma. The victim's ability to work, interact with the world, and perform daily activities can be severely impacted. In many cases, the victim may become completely dependent on others for their daily needs.

The loss of eyesight can also lead to social stigmatization, discrimination, and ostracism. It can make the victim more vulnerable to further abuse and violence, as they may become easy targets due to their inability to see or defend themselves.

In addition to the physical and emotional consequences, the victim may also require long-term medical treatment, including ophthalmologic care, vision rehabilitation, and psychological counseling. However, such treatments can be expensive, and many survivors cannot afford them.

- **Fate worse than death:**

In the context of acid attacks, the phrase "fate worse than death" is often used to describe the extreme and lifelong consequences that victims of these attacks face. The physical and emotional trauma of an acid attack can be devastating, leaving victims with permanent disfigurement, blindness, and other disabilities.

Acid attacks not only cause physical harm but also emotional and psychological trauma that can last a lifetime. Victims of acid attacks may experience a loss of self-esteem, depression, anxiety, and post-traumatic stress disorder (PTSD). They may also face social isolation, stigma, and discrimination, making it difficult for them to reintegrate into society.

In addition to the physical and emotional trauma, acid attacks can also impact victims' economic well-being. Many survivors are unable to work or pursue their careers due to their injuries, leaving them with financial difficulties and relying on the support of their families or the state.

The phrase "fate worse than death" is used to emphasize the severity of the consequences that acid attack victims face. It highlights the need for stronger legal and social support for the survivors, including medical treatment, psychological counseling, and economic rehabilitation. It also underscores the need for greater efforts to prevent acid attacks from happening in the first place.

3

The IPC & Acid Attacks

The Indian Penal Code (IPC) provides legal provisions to deal with acid attacks as a form of violence. Acid attacks are considered a heinous crime and carry severe punishments under the IPC.

Here are the sections of the IPC that deal with acid attacks:

- **Section 320:**

Section 320 of the Indian Penal Code (IPC) deals with the definition of hurt and the types of injuries that fall under it. The section provides a list of injuries that are considered hurt and categorizes them into two types - simple hurt and grievous hurt. Simple hurt refers to injuries that do not cause any lasting harm to the victim, while grievous hurt refers to injuries that result in permanent disfigurement or endanger the victim's life.

In the case of acid attacks, the injuries suffered by the victim fall under the category of grievous hurt. The use of acid as a weapon causes severe and lasting damage to the victim, including permanent disfigurement and loss of eyesight. As per Section 320 of the IPC, acid attacks are classified as grievous hurt, and the perpetrators are liable for imprisonment for up to seven years.

The Criminal Law Amendment Act of 2013 added a new section, Section 326A, to the IPC, which specifically deals with acid attacks. The section defines acid attacks as a form of grievous hurt and provides for stricter punishment for the offenders. The Act stipulates that anyone convicted of an acid attack can be imprisoned for a term ranging from ten years to life imprisonment, along with a fine.

Section 320 of the IPC provides the legal framework for defining hurt and categorizing the types of injuries that are punishable under the law. Acid attacks, which cause permanent disfigurement and loss of eyesight, fall under the category of grievous hurt and are punishable under the IPC. The Criminal Law Amendment Act of 2013 further strengthened the legal provisions related to acid attacks by introducing Section 326A to the IPC and providing for stricter punishment for the offenders.

- **Section 322:** Section 322 of the Indian Penal Code deals with voluntarily causing of hurt. It states that whoever voluntarily causes hurt shall be punished with imprisonment of either description for a term which may extend to one year, or with fine which may extend to one thousand rupees, or with both. However, if the hurt caused is grievous, the punishment may extend up to seven years of imprisonment and/or fine.

In the case of acid attacks, the offense of voluntary causing of hurt is replaced by the more severe charge of voluntarily causing grievous hurt. This is because acid attacks cause severe injuries and disfigurement, often leading to lifelong physical and emotional trauma for the victim. The punishment for this offense can range from 10 years to life imprisonment.

- **Section 326A:** Section 326A of the Indian Penal Code was introduced through the Criminal Law Amendment Act, 2013, and it deals specifically with acid attacks. This section defines the offence of causing grievous hurt by throwing or administering acid.

According to Section 326A, whoever causes permanent or partial damage or deformity to any part of the victim's body through acid attack shall be punished with imprisonment for a term which shall not be less than ten years but which may extend to imprisonment for life, along with a fine.

Additionally, the section also provides for enhanced punishment in case of a second or subsequent offence. If the offender has committed a second or subsequent offence under this section, then he/she shall be punished with imprisonment for life which shall mean imprisonment for the remainder of that person's natural life, along with a fine.

This section is a significant step towards addressing the issue of acid attacks in India. It recognizes the severity of the crime and provides for strict punishment to the offenders. It also serves as a deterrent to potential offenders who may consider committing such a heinous crime. Overall, Section 326A plays an essential role in ensuring justice and protection to the victims of acid attacks.

This section deals specifically with acid attacks and states that anyone who causes permanent or partial damage or deformity to another person's face or body using acid can be punished with imprisonment for ten years to life and a fine.

- **Section 326B:** Section 326B of the Indian Penal Code was added by the Criminal Law (Amendment) Act, 2013. It deals with the offence of throwing or administering acid. The section states that whoever throws or attempts to throw acid, or uses any other means to administer acid on another person, shall be punished with imprisonment for a term which shall not be less than ten years but which may extend to imprisonment for life, and shall also be liable to fine.

The section further states that whoever voluntarily causes grievous hurt by throwing acid, or using any other means to administer acid on another person, shall be punished with imprisonment for a term which shall not be less than ten years but which may extend to imprisonment for life, and shall also be liable to fine. The section defines "grievous hurt" as any hurt which endangers life or which causes severe bodily pain or damage to any bodily organ.

The section also provides that if the acid attack results in the death of the victim, the offender shall be punished with death or imprisonment for life, and shall also be liable to fine.

Section 326B of the IPC deals with the offence of throwing or administering acid, and provides for stringent punishment for those who commit such heinous crimes. The section recognizes the severe physical and emotional trauma caused by acid attacks and aims to deter such crimes by imposing severe penalties on the offenders.

- **Section 354D:** Section 354D of the Indian Penal Code deals with the offence of stalking. It defines stalking as following a person, contacting or attempting to contact a person to foster personal interaction repeatedly despite clear indication of disinterest by such person, or monitoring the use by a person of the internet, email or any other form of electronic communication.

The section provides for punishment for the offence of stalking with imprisonment for a term which may extend to three years for the first-time offence, and with imprisonment which may extend to five years for subsequent offences.

The offence of stalking is a serious issue as it can lead to physical harm and mental trauma for the victim. The section aims to provide a legal remedy for victims of stalking and to deter potential offenders from engaging in such behaviour. It is important for the police and the judiciary to take the offence of stalking seriously and to ensure that victims receive the necessary protection and support.

- **Section 307 :** Section 307 of the Indian Penal Code deals with the offence of attempted murder. It states that any person who attempts to commit murder shall be punished with imprisonment for a term which may extend to ten years, and shall also be liable to a fine.

In the context of acid attacks, Section 307 may be invoked if the attacker had the intention to kill the victim but was not successful in doing so. If the victim sustains severe injuries and the attack was premeditated, the offender may be charged with attempted murder under Section 307.

However, in many cases of acid attacks, the intention of the attacker may not be to kill the victim but to cause permanent disfigurement or to exact revenge. In such cases, the offender may be charged under other sections of the IPC, such as Section 326A or 326B, which deal specifically with acid attacks.

- **Section 325:** Whoever, except in the case provided for by section 335, voluntarily causes grievous hurt, shall be punished with imprisonment of either description for a term which may extend to seven years, and shall also be liable to fine.

The section defines "grievous hurt" as any hurt which endangers life, causes the victim to be in severe bodily pain, or causes permanent disfigurement or any other injury that is likely to cause a permanent impairment of the victim's body or mind.

In the context of acid attacks, section 325 can be applied in cases where the acid attack has caused grievous hurt to the victim. The punishment for causing grievous hurt can be imprisonment for up to seven years, along with a fine. However, if the victim has been permanently disfigured or disabled, the punishment can be increased up to life imprisonment.

Section 325, along with other sections of the IPC such as 326A and 326B, provides legal protection to the victims of acid attacks and ensures that the offenders are held accountable for their actions. It is important for the victims of acid attacks to be aware of their legal rights and for the law enforcement agencies to ensure that the offenders are brought to justice.

The IPC provides a comprehensive framework to address acid attacks and bring the offenders to justice. The sections dealing with acid attacks highlight the severity of the crime and ensure that the offenders face severe punishments.

4

Causes / Reasons for Acid Attacks

Acid attacks are a heinous crime that has become a widespread social issue in India, with a sharp rise in incidents in recent years. The reasons behind this gruesome act are complex and varied, and are rooted in deep-seated societal problems such as gender inequality, the objectification of women, and the lack of effective laws and law enforcement.

The majority of the victims of acid attacks are women, and the attacks are often perpetrated by men as a form of revenge, punishment or coercion. Furthermore, many attackers use acid as a cheap and easily accessible weapon, which they can use to cause permanent physical and psychological harm to their victims.

This has resulted in a culture of fear, where women are afraid to speak out or report the crime, and often face ostracization from their families and communities. Addressing the root causes of acid attacks is crucial to prevent this heinous crime from being committed in the future, and creating a safe and just society for all.

- **Male Dominating Society:**

A male-dominated society refers to a social structure in which men have a disproportionate share of power and influence over women. This form of societal structure is based on patriarchal beliefs, which place men at the center of social, economic, and political power while relegating women to a subordinate and marginalized position. In such societies, men are expected to be the primary providers for their families, and women are expected to be submissive and obedient to male authority.

The male-dominated societal structure has its roots in deep-seated gender biases that have been reinforced over time through cultural and social practices. It is often associated with various forms of gender-based violence, including acid attacks, sexual harassment, domestic violence, and other forms of abuse.

In India, patriarchal beliefs and practices are deeply ingrained in the culture, and as a result, the country continues to struggle with issues of gender inequality and gender-based violence. Acid attacks are one of the most brutal forms of violence that women face in a male-dominated society like India.

This issue requires a concerted effort to challenge gender biases, promote gender equality, and ensure that the laws and policies protect the rights and dignity of women.

- **Inexpensive & Effortless obtainability of Acids:**

Another major cause of acid attacks in India is the inexpensive and effortless obtainability of acids. Acid is widely used in industries, agriculture, and households for various purposes, and it is easily available in the market.

However, the lack of regulation and control over the sale of acid makes it accessible to anyone, including those who may have malicious intent. The cheap cost of acid makes it an attractive weapon for those who cannot afford firearms or other lethal weapons. Additionally, the use of acid as a weapon is easy and does not require any special training or skill, making it an appealing choice for attackers.

- **Peer Jealously :**

Peer jealousy is one of the causes of acid attacks in India. It is a complex issue that arises when one individual feels inferior or threatened by the success, happiness, or well-being of another individual in their peer group. This feeling of jealousy can often lead to harmful behavior, such as an acid attack.

In many cases, acid attacks are a result of one person's jealousy towards another person's success, beauty, or happiness. The attacker may feel that they have been left behind in life, and they may want to destroy the life of the person they are jealous of. Acid attacks are seen as a way to achieve this goal as they can cause permanent damage to the victim's face and body, leaving them disfigured for life.

- **Domestic Violence :**

Domestic violence is a major contributing factor to acid attacks in India. In many cases, acid attacks are used as a tool for controlling and punishing women who resist or challenge patriarchal norms and gender roles within the household. This can include cases of domestic violence such as spousal abuse, dowry-related violence, and other forms of gender-based violence.

Women who are victims of domestic violence are often vulnerable to acid attacks because they are seen as challenging the male-dominated power structures that underpin their abuse. Acid attacks can be used as a means of punishing women who dare to resist or assert themselves in situations where they are expected to remain subservient to their husbands or partners.

In some cases, acid attacks are also used as a means of retaliating against women who have reported incidents of domestic violence to the authorities or sought legal recourse against their abusers. Acid attacks are seen as a way to silence women and prevent them from speaking out against their abusers.

Furthermore, many women who are victims of domestic violence are economically dependent on their abusers, making it difficult for them to leave and seek refuge elsewhere. Acid attacks can be used as a means of preventing women from leaving their abusers by permanently disfiguring them and making it difficult for them to find employment or remarry.

Domestic violence and acid attacks are closely linked in India, with acid attacks being used as a means of controlling and punishing women who resist patriarchal norms and gender roles within the household.

- **Lovers get rejected in proposing the girl/boy:**

Acid attacks often occur as a result of romantic rejection, particularly when a male partner's advances are rejected by a female partner. In such cases, the male partner may feel a sense of anger, frustration, and a need to control the woman's actions. In some cases, the male partner may resort to violence, including acid attacks, as a means of punishing the woman for rejecting him or as a way to assert his power and control over her.

In a male-dominated society, where women are often viewed as subordinate and subservient to men, male partners may feel that they have a right to control their female partners. When a female partner rejects their advances or threatens their sense of power and control, they may resort to violent means to regain that control. Acid attacks, in this context, are a particularly devastating and cruel form of violence, as they leave the victim with permanent disfigurement and trauma.

It is important to note that romantic rejection is not an excuse for violent or criminal behavior, and individuals who engage in such behavior should be held accountable for their actions.

- **Protect the Honours of family:**

The concept of "honour" in many cultures is heavily tied to the behavior and actions of women in a family. In some cases, men feel that they have the responsibility to protect the honour of their family by punishing women who they feel have brought shame or dishonour to the family. This can take the form of acid attacks, as a way to disfigure and punish women who are perceived to have acted in a way that has brought shame on their family.

In some cases, women who have been attacked with acid are blamed for bringing shame on their family, even if they are the victims of the attack. This reinforces the idea that women are responsible for the behaviour of men and that they must act in a certain way in order to protect the honour of their family.

It is important to challenge these harmful and patriarchal ideas, and to promote gender equality and respect for women as individuals with their own agency and autonomy. Women should not be held responsible for the behaviour of men and should be free to live their lives without fear of violence or retribution.

5

Outcomes of Acid Attacks

Acid attacks have severe physical and emotional consequences on the victims. The corrosive nature of the acid can cause permanent disfigurement and scarring of the face, neck, and other exposed body parts. It can also lead to the loss of eyesight and other sensory functions, permanent disability, and in extreme cases, even death. Survivors often face significant challenges in their personal and professional lives due to the physical and psychological trauma of the attack. They may require extensive medical treatment, including multiple surgeries, to regain their appearance and mobility. Acid attack survivors also face social stigma, discrimination, and isolation due to their disfigurement, leading to psychological distress and reduced opportunities for education, employment, and social interaction. The impact of acid attacks on the victims and their families is profound, with long-lasting physical, psychological, and social consequences.

- **Physical Effect** : Acid attacks can cause severe and permanent physical damage to the victim. The acid can burn and melt the skin, disfigure the face and body, and cause blindness, deafness, and loss of limbs. The severity of the physical effects depends on the strength of the acid, the duration of the exposure, and the parts of the body affected.

The victim may suffer from excruciating pain, shock, and infection. The acid can also cause scarring, contracture, and keloids, which can limit the victim's mobility, cause deformity, and affect their self-esteem and confidence. In some cases, the victim may need multiple surgeries and lifelong medical care, which can be financially and emotionally draining.

The physical effects of acid attacks can also lead to social and economic consequences. The victim may face discrimination, isolation, and stigma from the society. They may be unable to work or study, and may become dependent on their family or the government for support. The physical effects of acid attacks can, therefore, have a profound and long-lasting impact on the victim's life.

- **Psychological Effect:**

The psychological effects of acid attacks can be severe and long-lasting. Survivors often experience anxiety, depression, post-traumatic stress disorder (PTSD), and a range of other psychological problems. The trauma of an acid attack can lead to a loss of self-esteem and confidence, social isolation, and difficulty in trusting others.

Acid attack survivors may also experience feelings of shame, guilt, and anger, and may have difficulty coming to terms with the physical changes to their appearance. The disfigurement caused by acid attacks can affect a person's sense of identity and self-worth, leading to long-term emotional and psychological distress.

In addition to the psychological effects on the survivors, acid attacks can also have an impact on their families and communities. Family members may experience guilt, anger, and sadness, and may have to provide ongoing care for the survivor. Communities may also stigmatize the survivor, leading to further isolation and psychological distress.

- **Social & Economic Effects:**

Acid attacks not only have physical and psychological effects but also have a significant impact on the social and economic well-being of the victim. Acid attacks can leave the victim with permanent disfigurement, making it difficult for them to continue their usual social activities or work. The victim may feel socially isolated and face discrimination and prejudice from society, leading to a loss of self-esteem and confidence. They may be ostracized by their family, friends, and community.

The social and economic impact of acid attacks also includes the cost of medical treatment, rehabilitation, and lost income due to disability or inability to work. The victim may require multiple surgeries and prolonged medical care, leading to a significant financial burden on them and their family.

In addition to the direct impact on the victim, acid attacks also affect their families, who may have to provide emotional and financial support. The families of the victim may also face social stigma and discrimination from society. Some people do suicide because of lack of the social support.

Overall, the social and economic impact of acid attacks is significant and long-lasting, affecting not only the victim but also their families and communities.

ᑭᑭᑭ

6

Landmark Judgements

- **Laxmi v. U.O.I.**

Laxmi v. Union of India is a landmark case in India that was filed by Laxmi, an acid attack survivor, in the year 2006. Laxmi was attacked with acid when she was 15 years old by a man who was over twice her age. The attack left her disfigured and traumatized.

Laxmi filed a petition in the Supreme Court of India seeking compensation from the government, regulation of acid sales, and rehabilitation of acid attack survivors. The petition also sought to bring the issue of acid attacks to the forefront and to make the government and society more aware of the problem.

The case resulted in the Supreme Court issuing guidelines to regulate the sale of acid and to provide better support and rehabilitation to acid attack survivors. The guidelines prohibit the sale of acid to anyone below the age of 18 and require sellers to maintain a record of the sale of acid, including the details of the buyer.

The court also ordered the central and state governments to provide free medical treatment and compensation to the victims of acid attacks. Additionally, the court ordered the establishment of fast-track courts to ensure speedy trials in acid attack cases. The case not only brought the issue of acid attacks to the forefront but also resulted in the government and society taking the problem seriously. The case brought to light the need for better laws and regulations to protect the rights of acid attack survivors and prevent such attacks from happening in the future.

Overall, Laxmi v. Union of India is a significant case that highlights the need for better support and rehabilitation for acid attack survivors and the importance of bringing the issue of acid attacks to the forefront of public discourse.

- **Parivartan Kendra v. U.O.I & Ors.**

Parivartan Kendra v. U.O.I & Ors. is a landmark case in the fight against acid attacks in India. The case was filed by Parivartan Kendra, a non-governmental organization that works towards the welfare of acid attack survivors.

The case was filed in response to the rising number of acid attacks in the country and the lack of effective measures to prevent such attacks and provide support to the victims. The petitioners in the case sought directions from the court to the government to take steps to regulate the sale of acid and provide better support and rehabilitation to acid attack survivors.

The court in its judgment recognized that acid attacks are a violation of the victim's fundamental right to life and personal liberty. The court noted that the sale of acid is largely unregulated in India, and anyone can purchase acid with little or no documentation.

The court ordered the government to take various steps to regulate the sale of acid and provide better support to acid attack survivors. Some of the key directions given by the court include:

1. **Regulating the sale of acid:** The court directed the government to require sellers to maintain a record of the sale of acid, including the details of the buyer. The court also directed the government to restrict the sale of acid to licensed sellers only and to prohibit the sale of acid to anyone below the age of 18.
2. **Compensation to victims:** The court directed the government to provide compensation to the victims of acid attacks, including medical treatment, rehabilitation, and monetary compensation.
3. **Rehabilitation:** The court directed the government to provide free medical treatment to the victims of acid attacks, including plastic surgery and post-operative care. Additionally, the court directed the government to provide vocational training and employment opportunities to help the victims lead a normal life.
4. **Fast-track courts:** The court directed the government to establish fast-track courts to ensure speedy trials in acid attack cases.

The judgment in Parivartan Kendra v. U.O.I & Ors. has been instrumental in bringing about significant changes in the regulation of the sale of acid and the support provided to acid attack survivors in India.

- **Sabana Khatun v. State of W.B. & Others:** Sabana Khatun v. State of W.B. & Others is a landmark case that was filed in the Supreme Court of India in 2011. The case brought attention to the issue of acid attacks in the country and the need to provide better support and rehabilitation to the victims. Sabana Khatun, the petitioner in the case, was a victim of an acid attack in 2009. She suffered severe burns on her face, neck, chest, and other parts of her body. She filed the case to seek compensation from the government and to highlight the need for better laws to regulate the sale of acid and provide support to the victims.

In its verdict, the Supreme Court directed the state governments to provide free medical treatment to the victims of acid attacks and to set up special cells to provide them with legal and financial aid. The court also ordered the central government to regulate the sale of acid and to make it mandatory for buyers to produce identification before purchasing acid.

The court's verdict in the Sabana Khatun case was a significant step towards addressing the issue of acid attacks in India. The case highlighted the need for better laws to regulate the sale of acid and provide support to the victims. The verdict also brought attention to the need for better rehabilitation and compensation for the victims of acid attacks.

- **Maqbool v. State of U.P. & Others**:

In the case of Maqbool v. State of U.P. & Others, the victim was a 16-year-old girl who had rejected the accused's marriage proposal. The accused threw acid on her face, which caused her to suffer severe injuries and permanent disfigurement.

The trial court had convicted the accused under Section 307 of the Indian Penal Code (attempt to murder) and sentenced him to seven years of imprisonment. However, the High Court reduced the sentence to three years.

The Supreme Court, in its judgment, held that the High Court had erred in reducing the sentence without any valid reason. The Court observed that acid attacks were a heinous crime and the punishment must be commensurate with the severity of the offence. The Court noted that the victim had suffered permanent disfigurement and psychological trauma as a result of the attack, and the punishment must serve as a deterrent to prevent such crimes from happening in the future.

The Court also directed the State government to pay compensation to the victim and provide her with adequate medical treatment and rehabilitation. The Court further directed the government to take steps to regulate the sale of acid and prevent its misuse. The judgment in this case is a significant step towards addressing the issue of acid attacks in India and providing justice and support to the victims.

- **Delhi Administration v. Mewa Singh:**

Delhi Administration v. Mewa Singh was a case that dealt with the issue of compensation for acid attack victims. In this case, Mewa Singh, a resident of Delhi, was attacked with acid by a group of people, causing him serious injuries and disfigurement. The case was brought before the Delhi High Court, which directed the Delhi Administration to pay compensation of Rs. 3 lakh to Mewa Singh for the medical expenses he had incurred and for the loss of his livelihood.

The Delhi Administration challenged this decision in the Supreme Court, arguing that it was not responsible for paying compensation in cases of criminal violence. However, the Supreme Court rejected this argument and upheld the decision of the Delhi High Court. The court observed that the state has a duty to protect its citizens and to provide them with adequate compensation in cases of violence, especially when the victim has suffered serious injuries and loss of livelihood.

The case of Delhi Administration v. Mewa Singh established an important precedent in the area of compensation for victims of acid attacks and other forms of violence. It affirmed the principle that the state has a duty to protect its citizens and to provide them with adequate compensation in cases of criminal violence.

7

Preventive Measures

Preventive measures refer to the steps taken to avoid or reduce the occurrence of a particular event or problem. In the case of acid attacks, preventive measures are crucial to reduce the incidence of this heinous crime. Preventive measures can be classified into three categories: primary prevention, secondary prevention, and tertiary prevention.

Primary prevention aims to prevent acid attacks from occurring in the first place by addressing the root causes of the crime, such as gender inequality, economic disparities, and access to acid. Secondary prevention focuses on identifying and intervening in cases where there is a high risk of an acid attack occurring.

Tertiary prevention aims to support victims of acid attacks, including medical treatment, rehabilitation, and reintegration into society. Preventive measures are essential to reducing the incidence of acid attacks and addressing the root causes of this crime.

- **Is it enough to make laws or start an NGO's for preventing this acid attacks?** Laws and NGOs are necessary to prevent acid attacks, but they may not be sufficient on their own. The root causes of acid attacks, such as gender-based violence, patriarchal attitudes, and lack of economic opportunities, need to be addressed to prevent such heinous crimes.

Laws are essential in deterring potential attackers and bringing the perpetrators to justice. The Acid Attacks and Prevention Act, 2013, mandates strict punishment for acid attacks, regulates the sale of acid, and provides for rehabilitation of victims. However, the implementation of these laws is often lax, and the victims do not receive timely justice. Therefore, there is a need for effective implementation of these laws to prevent acid attacks.

NGOs play a crucial role in supporting the victims of acid attacks, providing legal aid, medical treatment, and rehabilitation. They also conduct awareness campaigns to educate people about the severity of acid attacks and ways to prevent them. However, the number of NGOs working on this issue is limited, and their impact is often localized.

The prevention of acid attacks requires a concerted effort from the government, civil society, and individuals. The government needs to enforce the laws, create employment opportunities, and promote gender equality.

Civil society needs to raise awareness, provide support to the victims, and pressure the government to take action. Individuals need to question their patriarchal attitudes, respect women's autonomy, and be vigilant against potential attackers.

Therefore, while laws and NGOs are necessary, they need to be part of a comprehensive strategy to prevent acid attacks.

- **Steps to prevent this offence :** Preventing acid attacks is a complex issue that requires a multifaceted approach. Below are some steps that can be taken to prevent acid attacks:

1. **Regulation of Acid Sales:** Regulation of acid sales is one of the important steps towards preventing acid attacks. The unregulated sale of acid has contributed to the increasing number of acid attacks in India. The Supreme Court of India has issued guidelines to regulate the sale of acid and has also directed the central and state governments to implement them. These guidelines require the sellers of acid to maintain a register and provide information to the local police. The guidelines also prohibit the sale of acid to persons under the age of 18 and require the buyers to provide a valid identity proof.

The guidelines also suggest that the state governments should take steps to ensure that acid is only sold in licensed stores and restrict the sale of concentrated acid. The state governments are also directed to maintain a record of the sales of acid and take appropriate action against violators.

In addition to these guidelines, some state governments have also introduced laws to regulate the sale of acid. For example, the state of Bihar has banned the sale of acid without a license, while the state of Kerala has made it mandatory for sellers to maintain a register of buyers and take their photographs.

The regulation of acid sales is an important step towards preventing acid attacks. However, the implementation of these guidelines and laws needs to be ensured by the authorities. The public also needs to be made aware of the dangers of acid attacks and the laws and guidelines that have been introduced to prevent them. Only then can we hope to reduce the incidence of acid attacks in our society.

2. Awareness Campaigns: Awareness campaigns are a key strategy in the prevention of acid attacks. It is an effort to bring attention to the issue and educate the public on how to prevent these attacks. These campaigns can be organized by government agencies, NGOs, or other community organizations, and can take various forms, such as workshops, rallies, and social media campaigns.

The primary goal of an awareness campaign is to change attitudes and behaviors. It aims to create awareness about the consequences of acid attacks and the need to prevent them. An effective campaign can empower people to take action, such as reporting suspicious activities to the authorities or supporting the victims.

One example of a successful awareness campaign is the Stop Acid Attacks campaign, which was launched in India in 2013 by the Acid Survivors Foundation India (ASFI). The campaign aimed to raise awareness about acid attacks and provide support to survivors. It included a social media campaign, public rallies, and workshops to educate the public and law enforcement officials about the issue.

Another example is the Acid Survivors Foundation Pakistan, which has been working since 2006 to raise awareness about acid violence and to provide support to survivors. The organization runs a hotline for victims and has developed a comprehensive prevention program that includes awareness campaigns, support for victims, and advocacy for legal reform.

Awareness campaigns play a crucial role in preventing acid attacks. They can change attitudes and behaviors, empower people to take action, and provide support to survivors. These campaigns can be organized by government agencies, NGOs, or community organizations, and can take various forms. An effective awareness campaign is a vital component of any comprehensive strategy to prevent acid attacks.

3. **Rehabilitation and Support:** Rehabilitation and support for acid attack survivors is essential as the physical, psychological, and social impact of the attack can be long-lasting. Survivors need access to specialized medical treatment and psychological counseling to help them cope with the trauma of the attack.

Rehabilitation and support also involve addressing the social and economic impacts of the attack. Many survivors face difficulty in finding employment and are often ostracized by their community. Rehabilitation efforts must include vocational training, job placement, and legal assistance.

NGOs and government agencies play a crucial role in providing support to survivors of acid attacks. In India, NGOs such as Stop Acid Attacks, Acid Survivors Foundation India, and Chhanv Foundation have been at the forefront of providing rehabilitation and support to survivors. The government has also taken steps to provide financial and medical assistance to acid attack victims.

In addition to medical and legal support, rehabilitation efforts must also address the societal attitudes towards acid attack survivors. Education and awareness campaigns can help change the perception of survivors and increase empathy towards them. It is essential to create an environment where survivors are not stigmatized or discriminated against, and they can live their lives with dignity and respect.

Rehabilitation and support for acid attack survivors is a multi-faceted approach that involves medical treatment, psychological counseling, vocational training, legal assistance, and societal awareness campaigns.

4. **Fast-Track Courts:** Fast-track courts are specialized courts that are established to expedite the adjudication of specific types of cases, such as acid attack cases. These courts have been created to ensure that justice is delivered in a timely manner and that cases are resolved without undue delay.

Fast-track courts are designed to handle a large number of cases and dispose of them quickly. They have fewer adjournments, a simpler procedure, and a faster process of evidence recording. These courts are equipped with all the necessary tools and infrastructure required to ensure that cases are processed quickly and efficiently.

In the context of acid attack cases, fast-track courts can be particularly useful because of the complex and sensitive nature of such cases. The victims of acid attacks require immediate medical attention, and the psychological trauma that they experience can last a lifetime. By expediting the legal process, fast-track courts can help ensure that the victims of acid attacks receive the justice they deserve and can begin to rebuild their lives.

Fast-track courts are an important component of the legal system, and they play a crucial role in ensuring that justice is served. They are a valuable tool in the fight against acid attacks and are essential in ensuring that the victims of this horrific crime receive the support and assistance they need to rebuild their lives.

5. **Punishment:** The punishment for acid attacks in India has been increased in recent years, in response to the growing number of cases. The Acid Attacks and Prevention Act, 2013 mandates imprisonment of at least ten years, which can extend up to life imprisonment, for anyone convicted of an acid attack. The offender may also be fined and ordered to pay compensation to the victim. The fine amount must be adequate to cover the medical expenses of the victim, which can be substantial.

In addition, the Indian Penal Code (IPC) also has provisions for punishment for acid attacks under Sections 326A, 326B, 307, and 322. These sections prescribe imprisonment of varying periods, depending on the severity of the offence. For instance, Section 326A provides for imprisonment of at least ten years, which can extend up to life imprisonment, for causing grievous hurt by throwing acid. Section 326B provides for imprisonment of at least five years, which can extend up to seven years, for attempting to cause grievous hurt by throwing acid. Section 307 provides for imprisonment of at least ten years, which can extend up to life imprisonment, for attempt to murder by using acid. Section 322 provides for imprisonment of up to seven years, and/or fine, for voluntarily causing hurt by means of acid.

The severity of the punishment reflects the gravity of the offence and serves as a deterrent for potential offenders. It is important that the law is strictly enforced and the offenders are brought to justice, to ensure that the victims are not left to suffer alone. The punishment, along with the other preventive measures, can help to prevent the occurrence of acid attacks and provide a safer environment for everyone.

6. **Empowering Women:** Empowering women is an essential aspect of preventing acid attacks. It involves creating a safe and equal environment for women to live and work in. Empowering women includes providing education and vocational training to women, promoting women's participation in politics and leadership roles, and addressing gender inequalities in society. It also involves strengthening laws that protect women's rights and ensure their safety, as well as promoting gender sensitivity and positive attitudes towards women. Empowering women can help prevent acid attacks by reducing the power imbalance between men and women, providing women with the tools to defend themselves against violence, and creating a society that values and respects women. It is important to empower women and create a society that is free of violence and discrimination.
7. **Gender Sensitization:** Gender sensitization is the process of increasing awareness and sensitivity towards gender issues, gender roles, and gender-based violence. It aims to address and reduce the gender biases and inequalities that exist in society by educating individuals and communities on gender-related issues. Gender sensitization is a crucial tool in preventing acid attacks and other forms of violence against women. It helps to sensitize people towards women's rights, their importance in society, and the negative impacts of gender inequality. Gender sensitization also plays a significant role in the rehabilitation and support of acid attack survivors by creating a supportive and inclusive environment for them. By promoting gender sensitization, individuals, communities, and institutions can work towards preventing acid attacks

and creating a safer and more equitable society for women.

8. **Victim Protection**: Victim protection refers to measures taken to ensure the safety, security, and well-being of individuals who have been victimized by crimes such as acid attacks. In the context of acid attacks, victim protection is a crucial element in the rehabilitation process, as victims often face physical, psychological, and social challenges. The protection measures include providing safe housing, medical assistance, counseling, and legal support.

Victim protection measures are implemented at various stages, starting from the time of the attack to the rehabilitation of the victim. During the first stage, the victim may require medical attention and emergency care. Victim protection personnel, including medical and legal professionals, can provide support to ensure that the victim receives proper medical attention and legal assistance.

During the rehabilitation process, the victim may require ongoing support and care. This can include providing safe and secure housing, counseling, education, and job training to help them become self-sufficient. In addition, legal assistance is also provided to help them pursue justice against the attacker.

Victim protection measures are important not only to support the victim but also to deter potential offenders. Knowing that there are measures in place to protect victims and hold attackers accountable can discourage individuals from committing such crimes.

Victim protection measures can help victims of acid attacks regain their lives and rebuild their confidence. These measures are an essential part of the overall effort to prevent acid attacks and ensure justice for the victims.

- **Legal apparatus should improve:**

The legal apparatus for acid attack cases in India has undergone significant changes in recent years. The Acid Attacks and Prevention Act, 2008 was enacted to specifically address acid attack cases and provide appropriate legal recourse to victims. However, there are still several challenges that need to be addressed in order to improve the legal apparatus for acid attack cases.

One major issue is the lack of specialized courts to handle acid attack cases. Though the 2008 Act mandates that such cases be heard by fast-track courts, the implementation of this provision has been poor in many parts of the country. This results in delays in the trial process and denies justice to victims who are already traumatized by the attack.

Another issue is the need to sensitize the police and judiciary about acid attack cases. Often, the police and judiciary may not take the case seriously or may not be aware of the specific legal provisions for acid attack cases. This results in poor investigation and prosecution of cases, which is detrimental to victims seeking justice.

There is also a need to strengthen victim protection mechanisms in acid attack cases. Victims may be subjected to social stigma, discrimination, and even violence. The state must take measures to ensure that the victim's identity is protected and that they are provided with adequate support, including legal aid, medical treatment, and counseling.

Lastly, there is a need to strengthen legal provisions to regulate the sale and distribution of acid. Despite the

Supreme Court's direction to regulate acid sales and the implementation of various state-level regulations, acid is still easily available in many parts of the country. The regulation of acid sales and distribution can go a long way in preventing acid attacks from taking place.

Overall, the legal apparatus for acid attack cases must improve to ensure that victims receive justice and are protected from future harm. This requires the effective implementation of existing laws and the introduction of new measures where necessary.

- **Government should take more corrective measures on the sale of acid:**

Acid attacks have become a serious issue in India, and it is imperative that the government takes necessary corrective measures to regulate the sale of acid. The easy availability of acid is one of the major reasons for the increase in acid attacks. Acid is easily available at local shops and is also sold in small quantities. This makes it easy for anyone to purchase acid, even without providing any identification proof.

The government can take several steps to regulate the sale of acid. One of the most effective measures would be to make it mandatory for sellers to maintain records of the sale of acid. This will help in tracking the sale of acid and also in identifying the buyers of the acid.

The government can also regulate the sale of acid by making it mandatory for sellers to obtain a license before selling acid. The license can be issued only after conducting a background check of the seller. This will help in identifying the sellers who are involved in the illegal sale of acid.

Another measure that can be taken by the government is to ban the sale of acid in open markets. The sale of acid can be restricted to authorized shops only, and it can be sold only to those who provide valid identification proof.

Apart from these measures, the government can also impose heavy penalties on those who are involved in the illegal sale of acid. The government can also conduct regular checks on shops selling acid to ensure that they are not involved in the illegal sale of acid.

Regulating the sale of acid is one of the most effective ways to prevent acid attacks. The government must take necessary corrective measures to ensure that acid is sold only to those who have a valid reason to purchase it, and it is not misused for criminal activities.

- **The shopkeeper should maintain a register that to whom it is sold and in how much quantity?**

One of the measures to prevent acid attacks is to regulate the sale of acid. As part of this, it has been suggested that shopkeepers should maintain a register of acid sales, which would include details such as the quantity sold and to whom it was sold. This would enable better tracking and monitoring of acid sales, making it easier to identify potential misuse or illegal sales.

By maintaining a register, shopkeepers can be held accountable for any acid sales that are used for malicious purposes. This can act as a deterrent and encourage them to exercise caution when selling acid to customers. Additionally, authorities can periodically check the registers to ensure that sales are being made in compliance with regulations.

However, it is important to note that merely maintaining a register may not be enough to prevent acid attacks. It needs to be accompanied by other measures such as strict regulation and licensing of acid sales, awareness campaigns, victim support and rehabilitation, and legal reforms.

- **Offence should be tried in short span of time:**

Offence of acid attack is a heinous crime that leaves the victim with physical, emotional, and psychological scars. To ensure justice to the victim, it is important that the case is tried in a short span of time. Delayed trials lead to the victim's trauma being prolonged, and the accused also may get an opportunity to evade the trial by threatening or bribing the victim.

Fast-track courts have been established to ensure speedy trials and quick disposal of acid attack cases. The Acid Attacks and Prevention Act, 2013 mandates the courts to complete the trial of an acid attack case within three months of the chargesheet being filed. The Act also states that the appeal process in such cases should be completed within three months from the date of filing the appeal.

However, in reality, the disposal of acid attack cases still takes a long time due to various reasons like lack of evidence, inadequate investigation, etc. Therefore, there is a need for the judicial system to take stringent measures to ensure the speedy disposal of acid attack cases. This can include training of judges, prosecutors, and investigating officers, setting up more fast-track courts, and ensuring that the trial process is not hindered due to any external influence or pressure.

The quick disposal of cases will not only ensure justice to the victim but will also send a strong message to the society that such crimes will not be tolerated, and the perpetrators will be brought to justice swiftly.

- **Punishment should be severe:**

Punishment for acid attacks is governed by the Indian Penal Code (IPC) and other related laws. The severity of the punishment has been a matter of debate and criticism in recent times. In the past, acid attack offenders were often punished with leniency or received lower sentences, which has led to calls for stricter punishment.

In response to this demand, the government of India amended the IPC in 2013 to provide for a minimum punishment of 10 years imprisonment, which can be extended up to life imprisonment, along with a fine for acid attack offenders. The amendment also included provisions for compensation to be paid to the victim and for the establishment of fast-track courts to expedite trials.

However, despite these amendments, there are still concerns about the efficacy of the punishment for acid attacks. Many activists and organizations have called for even stricter punishment, including the death penalty, for those convicted of acid attacks. They argue that the lifelong trauma and disfigurement caused by acid attacks warrant such a severe punishment.

On the other hand, some argue that the death penalty is not a solution to the problem and may not be an effective deterrent. They point out that a better approach would be to focus on prevention and education, as well as providing support to victims and their families.

Ultimately, the severity of the punishment for acid attacks is a matter of debate and subject to change based on social, political, and legal developments.

8

Role of Police & Judiciary

- **Role of Police:**

The police play a crucial role in preventing and responding to acid attacks. They are responsible for enforcing laws related to the sale and purchase of acids, ensuring the safety and protection of victims, and investigating and prosecuting perpetrators of acid attacks.

One of the primary responsibilities of the police is to enforce regulations related to the sale and purchase of acids. They should ensure that only licensed sellers are allowed to sell acids and maintain records of the quantity sold and to whom it was sold. The police should also conduct regular checks to ensure that the sellers are complying with the regulations and taking appropriate measures to prevent the misuse of acids.

In case of an acid attack, the police must respond promptly and ensure that the victim receives immediate medical attention. They must ensure the safety of the victim and their family, provide them with legal and psychological support, and investigate the case in a sensitive and professional manner. It is important that the police take into consideration the social and cultural factors that may have led to the attack and take appropriate steps to prevent such incidents in the future.

The police should also work closely with civil society organizations and other stakeholders to create awareness and educate the public about the consequences of acid attacks. They should organize sensitization programs for their own personnel and provide them with specialized training on handling acid attack cases. It is also important that the police work in collaboration with other government agencies to provide victims with rehabilitation and support services.

Overall, the police play a crucial role in preventing and responding to acid attacks. They must ensure that appropriate measures are taken to prevent the misuse of acids, and in case of an attack, they must respond promptly, investigate the case professionally, and provide the victim with adequate support and protection.

- **Role of Judiciary:**

The role of the judiciary in combating acid attacks is of paramount importance. The judiciary plays a crucial role in the prosecution of the accused and the dispensation of justice to the victims. The judiciary also ensures that the laws are implemented and that the guilty are punished accordingly.

In acid attack cases, the judiciary ensures that the trial is conducted in a fast and efficient manner. The judiciary also ensures that the victims are given a fair hearing and that their rights are protected. It also ensures that the accused are given a fair trial and that they are punished in accordance with the law.

In addition to this, the judiciary also has the power to interpret the law and make necessary changes to improve the legal framework for acid attack cases. This includes making recommendations for stricter laws and punishments to deter future offenders.

The judiciary also has a role to play in ensuring that victims of acid attacks receive adequate compensation and rehabilitation. It can order the state or the accused to provide financial assistance and medical treatment to the victims.

Overall, the role of the judiciary in combating acid attacks is critical in ensuring that justice is served and that the victims are given the necessary support to recover and rebuild their lives.

9

Benefits Should be Given to Victims

Acid attacks not only have physical, emotional, and psychological impacts on the victim but also bring several financial setbacks. In most cases, the victim's life is completely shattered. The victim is left with the trauma of the incident and the physical scars that can cause lifelong disability. In addition to the physical and mental health issues, the victim may have to deal with the financial burden of medical bills, rehabilitation costs, and loss of income due to the inability to work.

To help acid attack survivors cope with these challenges, various organizations and government bodies have taken initiatives to provide them with benefits and support. These benefits include financial aid, medical treatment, rehabilitation, and legal support. The Indian government has launched several schemes for acid attack survivors, including free medical treatment and compensation.

Several non-governmental organizations (NGOs) have also come forward to provide aid to acid attack victims. These organizations provide legal support to the victims, help them find employment, and provide counseling to help them cope with the trauma of the attack.

The benefits provided to acid attack survivors not only help them but also create awareness about the issue and encourage the society to be more empathetic towards the victims. By providing support and aid to the survivors, we can create a more inclusive and compassionate society that cares for its citizens.

- **Financial Compensation:**

Financial compensation is a form of payment that is awarded to an individual or group in recognition of a loss, injury, or damage suffered by them. In the case of acid attack victims, it is a necessary measure to help them in their rehabilitation process.

Financial compensation is awarded to acid attack victims in India under the Victim Compensation Scheme. This scheme was introduced by the Ministry of Home Affairs in 2015 as a part of the Criminal Law Amendment Act. The scheme is designed to provide monetary relief to victims who have suffered injuries due to violent crimes, including acid attacks.

The compensation amount varies depending on the severity of the injuries suffered by the victim. In the case of acid attack victims, the compensation ranges from Rs. 3 lakhs to Rs. 7 lakhs. However, this amount is not enough to cover the medical expenses, rehabilitation costs, and other losses incurred by the victim.

The government has also introduced various schemes to support acid attack victims financially. The Nirbhaya Fund was set up in 2013 to support initiatives aimed at enhancing the safety and security of women in India. The fund can be used to provide financial assistance to acid attack victims for their medical treatment, rehabilitation, and livelihood support.

In addition to this, various NGOs and organizations have come forward to support acid attack victims. They provide financial assistance for medical treatment, legal aid, and vocational training to help them become self-sufficient. Some organizations also provide shelter to victims who are facing financial difficulties.

Financial compensation is an essential measure to support acid attack victims. However, the compensation amount needs to be increased to cover the significant losses incurred by the victims. The government and NGOs should work together to provide financial support to acid attack victims and help them in their rehabilitation process.

- **Social help & Support -**

Social help and support are crucial for victims of acid attacks to cope with the physical and psychological trauma caused by the attack. The victims need support from their family, friends, and society as a whole. It is essential to create a supportive environment that helps them in their recovery.

The government and NGOs can play an active role in providing social support to victims of acid attacks. They can provide counseling and rehabilitation services to help victims deal with the psychological and emotional trauma caused by the attack. They can also offer assistance in finding employment, housing, and education opportunities to help them rebuild their lives.

Social support can also come from the larger community. The society can offer a non-judgmental and supportive environment for victims to recover and rebuild their lives. The media can play a critical role in creating awareness about the issue and highlighting the challenges faced by acid attack victims.

Overall, social help and support are crucial for the physical and mental recovery of acid attack victims. It is essential to provide them with a safe and supportive environment to help them move forward in life.

- **Rights of the Victim :**

Acid attacks not only cause physical, mental, and emotional trauma to the victims but also violate their basic human rights. In order to ensure justice for the victims, it is important to understand and recognize their rights. Some of the important rights of acid attack victims are:

1. **Right to medical treatment:** The right to medical treatment is one of the fundamental rights of every individual, including victims of acid attacks. When a person becomes a victim of an acid attack, the first step is to provide immediate medical treatment to minimize the physical harm caused by the attack. The treatment includes providing first aid, cleaning the wound, applying ointments, and dressing the wound.

The medical treatment should be provided at the earliest to avoid any complications and to ensure the proper healing of the wound. In some cases, the victim may need to undergo a series of surgeries to repair the damaged tissues and to reconstruct the affected body parts. The right to medical treatment also includes counseling and therapy to help the victim cope with the trauma and to prevent psychological disorders such as depression and anxiety.

It is the responsibility of the government and the society to ensure that every victim of acid attack has access to quality medical treatment, without any discrimination based on their financial status or social background. The government should also provide financial assistance to the victims to cover their medical expenses and to support them in their rehabilitation process.

The right to medical treatment is crucial for the victims of acid attacks to recover physically and mentally from the trauma. The government and the society should work towards ensuring that every victim has access to the necessary medical treatment and support to lead a dignified life.

2. Right to privacy: The right to privacy is a fundamental right of every individual, and it is enshrined in Article 21 of the Constitution of India. It is an essential right of a victim of acid attack who has already suffered a great deal of trauma, both physical and psychological. Victims of acid attacks often have to face a lot of public attention and curiosity which infringes on their privacy rights. Therefore, it is important to ensure that their privacy is protected by law.

To safeguard the privacy of victims of acid attacks, the courts have laid down several guidelines. For instance, the courts have directed that the identity of the victim should not be disclosed in the media, and any publication of the victim's photograph or other details should be done only after obtaining their express consent. Additionally, the courts have also directed that the trial of such cases should be held in camera (in private), so that the victim's privacy is not violated.

It is also important to ensure that the victim's medical records and other sensitive information are kept confidential, and are not shared with unauthorized persons. This is crucial for the victim's physical as well as psychological recovery. Moreover, in some cases, the victim may require special protection from the accused, and the state should take appropriate measures to provide the victim with security and protection.

The right to privacy is an essential right of every individual, including victims of acid attacks. It is important to ensure that their privacy is protected by law and appropriate measures are taken to safeguard their rights.

3. **Right to compensation:**

The right to compensation is an important right of the victim of an acid attack. The victim has the right to receive compensation for the physical, psychological, and emotional harm suffered as a result of the attack. Compensation helps the victim in the process of recovery and helps them to rebuild their lives.

In India, the Supreme Court has held that victims of acid attacks are entitled to compensation from the State or the attacker. The compensation should be adequate and commensurate with the injury suffered by the victim.

The compensation can be given to the victim in the form of monetary compensation, free medical treatment, and rehabilitation services. The State Government and the Central Government have various schemes and programs to provide compensation to the victims of acid attacks.

For example, the Central Government has set up the Nirbhaya Fund, which provides financial assistance to victims of acid attacks for medical treatment, rehabilitation, and other support services. The State Governments have also set up similar schemes and programs to provide compensation to the victims of acid attacks.

It is the duty of the State to ensure that the victim of an acid attack receives adequate compensation and support. The compensation should be given to the victim without delay and should be sufficient to cover the medical expenses, loss of earnings, and other expenses incurred by the victim.

4. **Right to education:** The right to education is a fundamental right of every individual, including the victims of acid attacks. It is important to ensure that the victims have access to education and are not discriminated against on the basis of their appearance or disability resulting from the attack.

The Right to Education Act, 2009 provides for free and compulsory education to all children in the age group of 6-14 years. This Act also prohibits discrimination on the grounds of gender, caste, religion, and disability. Additionally, the Rights of Persons with Disabilities Act, 2016 provides for inclusive education for persons with disabilities, including those with facial disfigurement resulting from acid attacks.

Many organizations and NGOs have come forward to support the education of acid attack survivors. They provide scholarships, vocational training, and skill development programs to help them build their careers and become self-sufficient.

However, there is still a long way to go in ensuring that the victims of acid attacks have access to education without discrimination. It requires a collective effort from the government, NGOs, and society as a whole to ensure that their right to education is protected and fulfilled.

5. **Right to work:** One of the fundamental rights of a victim of acid attack is the right to work. After an acid attack, the victim may suffer from physical injuries, facial disfigurement, and other disabilities that may make it difficult for them to find and maintain employment. The right to work ensures that victims have equal access to job opportunities and are not discriminated against on the basis of their physical appearance or disability.

The right to work is recognized in various international and domestic laws, including the Universal Declaration of Human Rights, the International Covenant on Economic, Social and Cultural Rights, and the Indian Constitution. In India, the Persons with Disabilities (Equal Opportunities, Protection of Rights and Full Participation) Act, 1995, also provides for the right to work and employment for persons with disabilities, including acid attack survivors.

To ensure that acid attack survivors can exercise their right to work, various measures can be taken. Employers can be sensitized about the issue and encouraged to hire survivors. Training and vocational programs can also be provided to enhance the employability of survivors. Additionally, laws and policies can be enacted to provide affirmative action and reservation in employment for acid attack survivors and other persons with disabilities.

Overall, the right to work is an important aspect of rehabilitation and reintegration for acid attack survivors. It allows them to live with dignity and independence and contribute to society.

6. **Right to security:** The right to security is a fundamental right of every individual, including acid attack victims. This right includes protection from physical harm and the fear of harm, as well as the assurance of adequate safety measures from the government. Acid attack victims are often subjected to threats and intimidation, both from their attackers and their acquaintances. They may face the risk of further attacks or harm, especially if they do not receive adequate protection from the authorities.

In addition to physical security, acid attack victims also have the right to emotional and mental security. They may experience trauma, anxiety, and depression as a result of the attack, which can affect their overall sense of security. It is the duty of the government to ensure that they receive adequate mental health support and counseling to help them cope with the aftermath of the attack.

The right to security also includes the right to access justice and seek legal remedies. Victims should have the right to file a complaint with the police and have their case investigated in a timely and efficient manner. They should also have access to legal aid and representation to ensure that their rights are protected and justice is served.

Overall, the right to security is essential for the well-being and dignity of acid attack victims, and the government has a responsibility to ensure that this right is upheld.

7. **Right to rehabilitation:** The right to rehabilitation is a crucial aspect of the rights of acid attack victims. Rehabilitation refers to the process of restoring or improving the physical, psychological, and social well-

being of the victim. It involves providing necessary medical care, psychological support, and vocational training to help the victim reintegrate into society.

Acid attack victims often suffer from physical and psychological trauma that can severely impact their ability to lead a normal life. They may require extensive medical treatment, including multiple surgeries and long-term rehabilitation. Moreover, they may also experience social stigma and discrimination, making it difficult for them to find employment or reintegrate into society.

The right to rehabilitation includes access to medical treatment and psychological support. This may involve specialized treatment and therapy to address physical injuries, including skin grafts, reconstructive surgery, and physiotherapy. Psychological support may include counseling, therapy, and support groups to help the victim cope with the trauma of the attack.

Additionally, the right to rehabilitation also includes access to vocational training and employment opportunities to help the victim become financially independent and reintegrate into society. This may involve providing job training, education, and support in finding employment.

The right to rehabilitation is essential to ensure that acid attack victims receive the necessary medical care, psychological support, and vocational training to help them reintegrate into society and lead a normal life. It is the responsibility of the government and society to ensure that these rights are protected and upheld.

8. **Right to justice:** Right to justice is one of the fundamental rights of every individual. It means that

every victim of an acid attack has the right to seek justice for the harm inflicted upon them. The right to justice encompasses several aspects, including access to the legal system, fair and speedy trials, and the opportunity to hold perpetrators accountable for their actions.

In the context of acid attacks, the right to justice includes access to specialized courts, such as fast-track courts, that are equipped to deal with such cases efficiently. It also involves ensuring that victims have access to legal aid and representation, and that they are not subjected to any discrimination or bias in the legal process.

The right to justice also includes holding perpetrators accountable for their actions, which requires effective investigation, prosecution, and punishment. This includes imposing appropriate penalties on those who commit acid attacks, as well as holding those who aid or abet the attack accountable.

Moreover, the right to justice involves providing support to victims throughout the legal process, ensuring that their rights are protected, and that they are not subjected to further harm or victimization. This includes providing psychological support, medical treatment, and rehabilitation services.

In conclusion, the right to justice is a critical component of ensuring that victims of acid attacks are able to recover from their injuries and lead fulfilling lives. It involves providing them with access to legal support, holding perpetrators accountable, and ensuring that they receive the support and services they need to recover from the attack.

It is important for the society to recognize and respect the rights of acid attack victims, and for the government to ensure that these rights are protected and upheld.

- **Art. 21 Right to Life & Personal Liberty:** Article 21 of the Indian Constitution guarantees the Right to Life and Personal Liberty to every individual. This includes the right to live with human dignity, the right to personal liberty, the right to freedom from torture, and the right to a fair trial. Acid attacks, which cause grievous harm and often lead to death, are a direct violation of Article 21.

The Supreme Court of India has held that the Right to Life under Article 21 includes the right to live with dignity, which is impossible after an acid attack. Victims of acid attacks face a lifetime of physical and emotional trauma, and the damage done to them cannot be undone.

The State has a duty to ensure that the Right to Life of every individual is protected, and that perpetrators of acid attacks are brought to justice. This includes providing medical treatment, psychological counselling, and financial compensation to victims of acid attacks. It also means that the State should take preventive measures, such as regulating the sale of acid and increasing awareness about the crime.

The Right to Life and Personal Liberty under Article 21 is a fundamental right that cannot be taken away, and it is the duty of the State to ensure that it is upheld. Acid attacks are a direct violation of this right, and the State must take all necessary measures to prevent them and ensure justice for the victims.

- **Should be supported mentally as well as physically:**

Yes, victims of acid attacks should be supported both mentally and physically. Acid attacks not only cause physical harm but also result in psychological trauma that can leave a lasting impact on the victim's mental health. Therefore, it is important to provide them with psychological counseling and support to help them cope with the trauma.

Physical support may include medical treatment, such as surgeries and skin grafts, to repair the damage caused by the acid. Financial support, such as compensation, can also help cover the costs of medical treatment and rehabilitation.

Mental support may include counseling, therapy, and support groups to help the victim deal with the emotional aftermath of the attack. This can help them to regain their confidence and self-esteem, and move forward with their lives.

Providing victims with both physical and mental support can help them recover from the traumatic experience of an acid attack and lead a normal life. It is the responsibility of society and the government to ensure that such support is readily available to those who need it.

- **How they feel:**

Victims of acid attacks often face a lot of difficulties and onerous situations in living in society. They may experience physical pain and scarring, which can lead to mental health issues such as anxiety and depression. They may also face social isolation, discrimination, and stigma. It can be difficult for them to find employment and access education or healthcare.

Additionally, they may feel unsafe and vulnerable, as the attack can have a lasting impact on their physical and emotional well-being. It is important to provide support and resources for these victims to help them overcome these challenges and rebuild their lives.

10

Acid Attacks Report

- **Acid attack in the year 2017 –**

In 2017, acid attacks continued to be a grave concern in India. Despite various measures taken by the government and NGOs to prevent such heinous crimes, the number of acid attacks remained high, and victims continued to suffer.

According to the National Crime Records Bureau (NCRB) report, there were 283 cases of acid attacks reported in India in 2017, which was a slight increase from the 2016 figure of 252. Out of the total cases, 70% of the victims were women. The majority of the attacks were committed in the northern states of Uttar Pradesh, Delhi, and Haryana.

The year also witnessed some horrific acid attack incidents that shook the entire nation. One such incident took place in the state of Uttar Pradesh, where a woman named Ritu Yadav was attacked with acid by two men on a bike. The incident took place in broad daylight, and the attackers managed to flee the spot. Ritu Yadav suffered severe burns on her face, chest, and hands and had to undergo multiple surgeries.

Another shocking incident took place in the state of Odisha, where a 22-year-old woman named Itishree Pradhan was attacked with acid by two men who had been stalking her for a while. Itishree suffered severe burns on her face and neck and had to undergo multiple surgeries. The incident led to widespread protests across the state, and the government was criticized for its failure to protect women.

The year also saw some positive developments in the fight against acid attacks. In April 2017, the Supreme Court of India directed all state governments to regulate the sale of acid and ensure that acid was only sold to individuals who possessed a valid license. The court also directed the government to provide free medical treatment and rehabilitation to acid attack victims.

NGOs and individuals also played a vital role in providing support and rehabilitation to acid attack victims. One such organization was Stop Acid Attacks, which continued to work tirelessly to provide medical and financial support to victims of acid attacks. The organization also worked to create awareness about acid attacks and advocated for stricter laws to prevent such crimes.

Despite the positive developments, the year 2017 highlighted the urgent need for stricter laws and stricter enforcement of existing laws to prevent acid attacks. The government and law enforcement agencies need to work together to ensure that acid attacks are not just punished but prevented altogether. Moreover, there is a need for a concerted effort by society to change attitudes towards women and to create a more gender-equal society where women are not viewed as objects to be attacked and maimed.

- **Acid attack in the year 2018 –**

In the year 2018, India witnessed a number of cases of acid attacks, indicating that despite strict laws and preventive measures, the heinous crime still exists. According to the Acid Survivors Foundation India, there were 200 reported cases of acid attacks in the country in 2018.

The report highlighted that majority of the victims were women and girls, who were attacked by jilted lovers, rejected suitors, or those seeking revenge. The states of Uttar Pradesh, West Bengal, and Delhi recorded the highest number of attacks, accounting for almost 50% of the total cases.

The report also revealed that despite strict regulations on the sale of acid, the substance was still easily accessible to perpetrators. In many cases, the acid was purchased from local hardware stores, often without any proper documentation or identification of the buyer.

The psychological impact of acid attacks on the survivors and their families was immense, with many victims suffering from depression, anxiety, and post-traumatic stress disorder. Additionally, the physical scars left by the attack often resulted in social isolation and economic marginalization, making it difficult for the victims to lead a normal life.

In terms of legal measures, the report noted that the fast-track courts set up to deal with acid attack cases were functioning effectively, with many cases being resolved within six months. However, the report also highlighted the need for better implementation of existing laws and the need for stricter punishment for the perpetrators.

The report also called for greater support and rehabilitation for the survivors, including access to free medical treatment, counseling, and financial assistance. The government was urged to take a more proactive role in this regard, and NGOs were urged to continue their efforts in providing support and advocacy for the victims.

The report highlights the need for continued efforts in preventing acid attacks, including stricter regulations on the sale of acid, greater awareness campaigns, and better support and rehabilitation for the survivors. It also highlights the need for a comprehensive approach that addresses the psychological, social, and economic impact of the crime on the victims and their families.

- **Acid attack in the year 2019 –**

Acid attacks have been a growing concern in India over the years. Despite the strict laws and regulations, these brutal attacks continue to take place, leaving the victims with life-long scars and trauma. In the year 2019, several such incidents were reported across the country, highlighting the need for more stringent measures to prevent and punish the perpetrators of such crimes.

One of the most shocking acid attacks in 2019 was reported in August in the state of Uttar Pradesh, where a 23-year-old woman was allegedly attacked by two men after she refused their advances. The victim suffered severe burn injuries to her face, chest, and hands, and had to undergo several surgeries to save her eyesight. The incident sparked outrage across the country, with people demanding strict action against the culprits and better safety measures for women.

Another disturbing incident was reported in July in the state of Telangana, where a 15-year-old girl was attacked with acid by a man who had been stalking her for months. The victim suffered burn injuries to her face and hands and had to be hospitalized for several weeks. The incident led to protests and demands for stronger laws to protect minors from such attacks.

In October, another acid attack was reported in the state of Bihar, where a 20-year-old woman was attacked by her boyfriend's brother after she refused to marry him. The victim suffered severe burns to her face and eyes and had to undergo several surgeries. The incident once again raised concerns about the growing trend of acid attacks as a means of revenge or intimidation.

Apart from these incidents, several other acid attacks were reported across the country in 2019, including in states like Maharashtra, Haryana, and West Bengal. These attacks not only leave the victims with physical scars but also cause long-lasting psychological trauma, affecting their ability to lead a normal life.

The government and various NGOs have been working to prevent such attacks and provide support to the victims. The Supreme Court has also taken note of the issue and has directed the states to regulate the sale of acid and provide better medical and legal assistance to the victims.

Acid attacks continue to remain a serious issue in India, with several incidents reported every year. The need of the hour is to implement more stringent measures to prevent such attacks, including better regulation of the sale of acid, stronger punishment for the perpetrators, and better support and rehabilitation for the victims. Only then can we hope to create a safer and more just society for all.

- **Acid attack in the year 2020:-**

Acid attacks continue to be a brutal reality in India, with several cases being reported in the year 2020. Despite increased awareness and stricter laws, acid attacks remain a prevalent issue in the country, and there is a need for continuous efforts to combat this heinous crime.

One of the most high-profile acid attack cases in 2020 was the attack on two sisters in Uttar Pradesh's Gonda district. The sisters were attacked with acid while they were asleep in their home. The attackers were known to the victims and had reportedly been harassing them for months. The incident sparked widespread outrage, and the police were quick to take action, arresting the accused within 24 hours of the attack.

Another shocking acid attack case was reported from Punjab's Patiala district, where a woman was attacked by her husband after she refused to give him money. The victim suffered severe burns on her face and other parts of her body, and she was rushed to the hospital in critical condition. The accused was arrested soon after the incident, and the victim's family members have demanded that he be given the harshest punishment possible.

In yet another disturbing incident, a 16-year-old girl was attacked with acid in West Bengal's Hooghly district. The victim had reportedly rejected a marriage proposal from the accused, who then attacked her with acid. The victim was admitted to the hospital with severe burns, and the accused was arrested soon after the incident.

Apart from these high-profile cases, there were several other acid attacks reported across the country in the year 2020. These incidents serve as a grim reminder of the need for stricter laws and better enforcement to prevent such heinous crimes from taking place.

In response to the rising number of acid attacks, several initiatives were taken by the government and NGOs to raise awareness and provide support to the victims. The government has set up fast-track courts to ensure speedy trials and has also introduced stricter regulations for the sale and purchase of acid. NGOs and social organizations have been working tirelessly to provide medical and emotional support to the victims and to create awareness about the issue.

While there have been efforts to combat acid attacks in India, the continued occurrence of such incidents shows that more needs to be done. Stricter laws, better enforcement, and increased awareness are necessary to put an end to this heinous crime and ensure that the victims get the support they need.

- **Acid attack in the year 2021:-**

As of August 2021, there have been numerous reports of acid attacks in India. Despite the efforts to curb the practice, the menace of acid attacks continues to haunt the country. The year 2021 has witnessed a rise in such incidents, despite the COVID-19 pandemic and nationwide lockdowns.

One of the most notable cases that came to light this year was the acid attack on three sisters in Uttar Pradesh's Gonda district. The attackers allegedly targeted the sisters because they refused to withdraw a complaint against them for eve-teasing. The sisters suffered severe burn injuries on their faces, necks, and hands.

In another incident, a woman in Delhi's Karawal Nagar was attacked with acid by her husband after she refused to return to him. The victim suffered burn injuries on her face and neck and was admitted to a nearby hospital.

A 24-year-old woman was also attacked with acid in Hyderabad by a man who had been stalking her for months. The victim, who was on her way to work, was rushed to a nearby hospital for treatment.

These incidents highlight the need for stricter laws and better implementation to prevent acid attacks in India. Despite the Supreme Court's guidelines and the government's efforts to regulate the sale and possession of acid, these incidents continue to occur, causing immense physical and psychological harm to the victims.

One positive development this year has been the Delhi High Court's order to the central government to amend the Indian Penal Code (IPC) to include acid attack as a separate offence. The court observed that acid attack is a heinous crime that requires harsher punishment than the current provisions under Section 326 of the IPC.

The court's order also directed the government to increase the compensation amount for acid attack survivors, noting that the current amount of Rs. 3 lakh was inadequate to cover the cost of medical treatment and rehabilitation.

Apart from the legal and policy changes, there is a need to create awareness and change the societal mindset towards acid attacks. The survivors of acid attacks face immense discrimination and stigma in society, which further adds to their trauma.

Non-profit organizations and civil society groups have been working towards creating awareness and providing support to the victims. However, their efforts need to be complemented by the government's initiatives to prevent such incidents from occurring in the first place.

The year 2021 has been witness to a rise in the number of acid attack incidents in India. While there have been some positive developments on the legal front, a lot more needs to be done to prevent such incidents and provide support to the survivors. It is the responsibility of all stakeholders, including the government, civil society, and individuals, to work together towards creating a safer and more inclusive society for all.

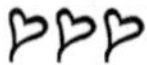

11

Guidelines given by Supreme Court of India

Acid attacks have become a rampant problem in India, causing grievous harm and disfigurement to the victims, mostly women. In an attempt to curb this heinous crime, the Supreme Court of India has issued several guidelines and directions to the Central and State Governments, police authorities, and other concerned bodies.

Here are some of the significant guidelines given by the Supreme Court of India to prevent and control acid attacks:

1. **Regulation of acid sales:** The Court directed the Central and State Governments to regulate the sale of acid and to prohibit the sale of acid to anyone below the age of 18. The guidelines also mandated that the shopkeepers must maintain a register of the sales, including the name and address of the buyer, the purpose of the purchase, and the quantity sold.
2. **Rehabilitation and support:** The Court ordered that the State Governments must provide free medical treatment, including reconstructive surgeries, to the

victims of acid attacks. They should also provide rehabilitation and support services such as counseling, vocational training, and financial aid.

3. **Awareness campaigns:** The Court directed the Central and State Governments to launch awareness campaigns on the dangers of acid attacks and their legal consequences. These campaigns should aim to educate the public and sensitize them towards the survivors of acid attacks.
4. **Gender sensitization:** The Court mandated that gender sensitization programs should be conducted for all police personnel and medical professionals. The training should focus on the importance of treating victims of acid attacks with sensitivity and empathy.
5. **Fast-track courts:** The Court directed that the cases of acid attacks should be tried in fast-track courts to ensure speedy justice. The guidelines also directed the State Governments to set up exclusive courts for the trial of acid attack cases.
6. **Punishment:** The Court ordered that the punishment for acid attacks should be severe and should include imprisonment of not less than 10 years and a fine. The guidelines also mandated that the compensation for the victims should be in proportion to the gravity of the crime and the harm caused.
7. **Empowering women:** The Court directed the Central and State Governments to take measures to empower women by providing them with education, employment, and skill development opportunities. The guidelines also mandated that the Governments should take steps to ensure the safety and security of women in public spaces.

8. **Victim protection:** The Court ordered that the victims of acid attacks should be provided with adequate protection and security. The guidelines mandated that the State Governments should provide police protection to the victims and their families if necessary.

The Supreme Court of India has issued several guidelines and directions to prevent and control acid attacks in the country. The implementation of these guidelines requires a collaborative effort between the Central and State Governments, police authorities, and other concerned bodies. The guidelines aim to provide comprehensive support and protection to the victims of acid attacks and to ensure that the perpetrators are brought to justice.

12

Suggestions

Acid attacks are heinous crimes that cause severe physical, emotional, and psychological trauma to the victims. Survivors of acid attacks are often left with permanent disfigurement, loss of vision, and severe pain. Even after the physical scars heal, the emotional and psychological trauma remains. Victims of acid attacks often find it challenging to cope with the aftermath of the attack, including social ostracism, employment discrimination, and financial difficulties.

To help acid attack survivors cope with their trauma and rebuild their lives, it is essential to provide them with appropriate medical care, rehabilitation, and support.

One of the most important ways to help acid attack victims is by providing them with immediate and quality medical care. Victims need prompt treatment to prevent further damage and complications. Medical treatment should include emergency first aid, surgical intervention, and rehabilitation.

Victims should receive emergency first aid to mitigate the immediate effects of the acid. Immediate treatment involves washing the affected area with water or saline to dilute the acid and remove it from the skin. The victim should then be rushed to the nearest hospital for medical attention. The hospital should have a specialized team of doctors and nurses to provide emergency care.

Surgical intervention is critical to minimizing the physical damage caused by acid. The surgery may involve skin grafting or reconstructive surgery to repair damaged tissue. Acid attack victims may require multiple surgeries to repair the damage caused by the acid.

Rehabilitation is also a crucial part of the treatment process. The victim may require physical therapy to regain strength and mobility. Counseling may also be necessary to help the victim cope with the emotional and psychological trauma.

Acid attack survivors often face financial difficulties due to the high cost of medical treatment and the loss of income resulting from the attack. To help them cope with the financial burden, it is essential to provide financial compensation and legal assistance.

Financial compensation can help victims cover the cost of medical treatment, rehabilitation, and lost income. The government should set up a compensation fund to provide financial assistance to acid attack victims. The compensation should be adequate to cover the victim's medical expenses and provide support for their livelihood.

Legal assistance is also essential to help acid attack survivors seek justice. Victims should be provided with free legal aid to help them file cases against the attackers. Legal aid should be provided at all stages of the legal process, including investigation, trial, and appeals. The legal system should ensure that cases are expedited and the accused are brought to justice.

Gender sensitization and awareness campaigns are crucial to changing societal attitudes towards women and ending violence against them. These campaigns can help educate the public on the consequences of acid attacks and raise awareness of the issue.

The government should launch awareness campaigns to sensitize people about the impact of acid attacks. These campaigns can help change the public's perception of acid attacks and encourage them to report any such incidents.

To prevent acid attacks, there is a need to strengthen laws and regulations related to acid sales. The sale of acid should be strictly regulated, and acid should only be sold to those who have a valid reason to use it.

The government should also ensure that shopkeepers maintain a register of acid sales and keep records of the buyers' identity and purpose of purchase. Shopkeepers who sell acid to unauthorized buyers should be penalized.

Empowering acid attack victims is critical to help them regain control of their lives. The government should provide victims with vocational training and employment opportunities to help them become financially independent.

Additionally, counseling and emotional support should be provided to help victims cope with the trauma and rebuild their self-esteem. Counseling can help victims overcome the emotional and psychological trauma caused by the attack and enable them to move on with their lives.

13

Conclusion

Acid Attack is a very Heinous Crime. It is a gender based crime. It is an offence in which a person throws an acid to harm/injured another person's face/eyes. It causes a severe pain, permanent disfigurement of eyes/face, infections or can even blind by this offence. Victim of Acid Attack can be anyone, he may be anyone a boy or a girl. They need support of society, of their family, they have also right to enjoy life in the way they want, society should not stop them for doing this. They need a physical, mental, social or economical support as they deserve that and they have right to take.

Here are some reasons why a holistic approach is necessary:

1. **Comprehensive medical treatment:** A holistic approach to supporting acid attack victims involves providing comprehensive medical treatment, including surgical procedures, skin grafts, and physical therapy. It also addresses the long-term effects of acid attacks, such as scarring and disfigurement.
2. **Emotional and psychological support:** Acid attacks can have long-lasting effects on the victim's mental health,

including anxiety, depression, and post-traumatic stress disorder (PTSD). A holistic approach provides emotional and psychological support to help victims cope with the trauma and move forward with their lives.

3. **Legal and financial support:** Acid attack victims may require legal and financial assistance to navigate the legal system and seek compensation for their injuries. A holistic approach provides support in these areas, including legal representation and financial assistance.
4. **Rehabilitation and reintegration:** Acid attack victims may face challenges in reintegrating into society, such as discrimination, stigmatization, and isolation. A holistic approach provides rehabilitation and support to help victims rebuild their lives and reintegrate into their communities.

It is important for individuals, organizations, and the government to take action to support acid attack victims and prevent these heinous crimes from occurring. Here are some calls to action:

1. **Donate to organizations supporting acid attack victims:** There are several organizations around the world that provide medical, emotional, and legal support to acid attack victims. Consider donating to these organizations to support their work and help victims access the care they need.
2. **Advocate for stronger laws and policies:** Governments can play a critical role in preventing acid attacks by enacting and enforcing stronger laws and policies to regulate the sale and use of acid. Advocate for stronger laws and policies in your community and hold elected officials accountable for their actions.

3. **Raise awareness and educate others:** Educate yourself and others about the causes and consequences of acid attacks, and the resources available to support victims. Use social media and other platforms to raise awareness and educate others about this issue.
4. **Provide emotional and psychological support:** If you know someone who has experienced an acid attack, offer emotional and psychological support. Encourage them to seek professional help and connect them with support services in their community.
5. **Combat stigma and discrimination:** Acid attack survivors may face stigma and discrimination due to their physical appearance or disability. Take action to combat stigma and discrimination in your community and support efforts to promote inclusivity and acceptance.

Supporting acid attack victims requires a collective effort from individuals, organizations, and the government. By taking action, we can help victims access the care and support they need, prevent future attacks, and create a more just and compassionate society.

References

- Deb,A and Chowdhury P. Roy , "A Fate Worse than Death: A Critical Exploration of Acid.Attack Violence in India", Law Mantra, Vol. 2, Issue 5, http://journal.lawmantra.co.in
- Mohapatra, Chinmaya Kumar and Nanda, Hiranmaya, "Acid Attack and Women in India: A Critical Analysis", Global Journal for Research Analysis, Vol. 4, Issue 7, July 2015.
- Nehaluddin, Ahmad, (2011), "Acid Attacks on Women: An Appraisal of the Indian Legal Response", 12 Asia-Pac. J. on Hum. Rts. & L. 55 2011.
- Menon Parvathi and Vashishtha Sanjay, (2013), Vitriolage & India – The Modern Weapon of Revenge, International Journal of Humanities and Social Science Invention, Volume 2 Issue 10, available at http://www.ijhssi.org/papers/v2(10)/Version-2/A0210020109.pdf.
- Kamakar, Rabindra Nath, (2006), Forensic Medicine and Toxicology: Theory, Oral & Practical, Academic Publishers, 1st. ed.
- Report of the Committee on Amendments to Criminal Law (Justice Verma Committee Report).
- The Criminal Law (Amendment) Act, 2013, Ministry of Law and Justice,
- Universal's Compendium Reports of the Law Commission of India, Vol. 18 (202nd to 234th Report), 2nd ed. 2010, Universal Law Publishing Co., New Delhi.
- Awasthi, Vanita and Gupta Rohit Kumar, "A Socio-Legal Study of Acid Attacks on Women in India", International

Journal of Research and Analysis, Vol. 2, Issue 6, 2015.

- Welsh, Jane, (2009), "IT WAS LIKE BURNING IN HELL", A thesis submitted to the faculty of the University of North Carolina
- https://cdr.lib.unc.edu/indexablecontent/uuid:e472922a-b4a3-47a4-82e5- 661dd7a966c5

9 798889 864936

Printed by Libri Plureos GmbH in Hamburg, Germany